MEMORY LANE
CREWE
INCLUDING NANTWICH
VOLUME FIVE

# By Gordon Davies

First published in Great Britain in 2005
by Gordon Davies of Crewe

© GORDON DAVIES 2005

ISBN 0-9550600-0-1

Printed and bound by Butler and Tanner
Frome, Somerset, England

# CONTENTS

# INTRODUCTION

THE English poet John Clare said a fond memory lost is like a friend forsaken. So how wonderful it is to bring those memories back and to once more enjoy the company of friends from long ago.

Few are the opportunities to do this and that is why Gordon Davies' Memory Lane books are so compelling. The old days in Crewe and Nantwich may be long gone but they are not forgotten. Among the many excellent photographs in this book will be some that, if only for a fleeting moment, reunite us with the people we lived, worked and played with in days gone by.

After four Crewe Memory Lane books, as well as Memory Lane Nantwich and Crewe Alex Remembered, one would have forgiven Gordon for saying that the well is dry and there are no more of these photographs. Far from it. Not only has he drawn on his extensive archive of pictures but people have responded to the previous books by offering more and, like fine wine. They seem to get better with age.

Not for nothing has Gordon been awarded a Mayor's Oscar by Crewe and Nantwich's 2004-05 Mayor, Steve Roberts, for the contribution his books have made to the community. Everyone who reads this book will find something which underlines why our memory always remembers the happy things.

I am delighted to see the old Crewe Carnival parade and pictures from the Rolls-Royce Field Day. The memories come flooding back when I see the Sandbach Ramblers football team which reached the heady heights of the old Cheshire League in the 1970s and Gordon Wallace making a presentation to a five-a-side team in 1968. He only made 93 appearances for Crewe Alex before injury cruelly cut short his career. Was he the finest player ever to pull on an Alex shirt?

It is also a joy to see the photograph of Petula Clark visiting Crewe Works in 1949. It opens a rich seam of memories of her and Jack Warner in The Huggets. More than half a century has gone by but the excitement in Nantwich when Wilf White and his horse Nizfella returned with a gold medal from the 1952 Helsinki Olympics is still obvious in the picture of that day.

These, of course, are just snippets from what is an impressive collection. Each reader will delight in unearthing his or her favourite nuggets from within this book. It will bring back memories you may well have thought you had lost and friends you have not forgotten after all.

Dave Fox
Editor, The Crewe Chronicle,
32-34 Victoria Street, Crewe

# ACKNOWLEDGEMENTS

Once again I would first like to thank Dave Fox, the editor of the South Cheshire Edition of The Crewe Chronicle, not only for his introduction to this book, but for the publicity he has provided for my previous books.

While many of the pictures in this book were photographed by me over many years, or taken from my stock of old pictures, I would like to thank the following people who have helped in the preparation by offering photographs or information, for which I am extremely grateful: Mike Yoxall Diane Betteley, H. Bullock, J. MacDonald, Frank Rhodes, Helga Armonies, Mrs Joan Elliott, Beryl Heaton, Gwen Thompson, Nelly Readdin, Peter Kent, Dennis and Betty Cornes, Tom Smith, Mary Oltram, Bentley Motors, Doreen Wain, Frank Dale, Linda Taylor, The Late Albert Hunn, Dave Lindop and Derek Baker.

My sincere apologies to anyone who has helped in any way but has not been included in these acknowledgements.

I dedicate this book to my sister Elva

# AROUND AND ABOUT IN CREWE

The London Dining and Tea Rooms on Nantwich Road in 1892, which also advertised rooms for cyclists, with Good Beds! Was this the forerunner of the Motel?

This certificate was awarded to Nellie Heath in June 1901 when she made a donation, of four shillings and five pence (22 pence), to the Crewe Memorial Cottage Hospital, to help with the funding of the Queen Victoria Ward for Children. The Memorial Cottage Hospital which stood on Victoria Avenue, was replaced with Leighton Hospital, which was opened by Queen Elizabeth 11 on 2nd May 1972.

A quiet Nantwich Road, looking towards Crewe Railway Station, in 1903.

Looking across the park lake towards the Queen's Park pavillion in 1904. The building was destroyed by arsonists in the 1970's.

Hightown, Crewe, in 1904. The shops enjoyed a passing trade in those days, but the area became isolated when the extension to West Street was opened in September 1980. Beckmount House to the right of the picture, later became the site of the Charlesworth Electrical business. The policeman on the left of the picture is carrying his heavy cape,- part of his uniform in those days. Note the street gas lighting to the right of the photograph; I don't think those glass bowls would last long these days! The shops verandah and the ornate roof facia was pulled down in the 1970's.

Nantwich Road 1904 at the junction of Gresty Road and Pedley Street. The Royal Hotel is on the right.

Nantwich Road in 1905, showing the Earl of Crewe Hotel on the left and garden walls on the right, which have now given way to a busy shopping area.

An idyllic scene in Queen's Park in the summer of 1906 when most of the trees were in their infancy.

West Street in 1907 with shops overflowing with goods it looked quite a busy shopping area in those days.

Staff outside the Crewe Co-operative Friendly Society Butchers Department, Broad Street in about 1910.

The Crewe to Shavington Crosville bus standing at the Newcastle Road level crossing in 1913. Note the solid tyres; rather an uncomfortable ride I would imagine. Still, even in those days, third class riding would have been better than first class walking!

Christ Church pictured in 1913; was built by the Grand Junction Railway Company and opened on 18th December 1845. The lich gate, to the right of the picture, was demolished some years ago; in 1977 the nave was deemed unsafe because of fungal decay and was also pulled down. That area of the church is now a remembrance garden. The chancel end of the church was re-designed and reopened for worship in 1979. The houses to the left of the picture were demolished in the 1960's and the present library was erected on the site. The cottages to the right of the church were pulled down and replaced with the present police station and large car parks..

St. Paul's Church, Hightown in 1915, looking regal, in the days when it still had its spire. The church closed in 1986; it is now a saleroom.

This stall was judged the best decorated during a competition at the Crewe Market to celebrate the Coronation of King George V1 in 1937. The lady nearest the camera is Edna Oliver, Mr Charlesworth is standing behind her. The name of the other lady is not known.

Mr F. Wood, third from left, with councillors and customers after winning the 'Best Stall' competition at the Crewe Market in 1938.

Looking across a busy Crewe Market Square towards Market Terrace, (now Queensway) in March 1938. The Market Square was the bus terminus until Crewe's first bus station opened in 1960.

The Empire Cinema which stood in Heath Street. This picture was taken in 1946; the commissioner is Mr Norman Tew and is seen here, in his summer uniform;- he wore a green long coat in the winter, - promoting the film "Night and Day", starring Jane Wyman, Cary Grant and Alexis Smith. The people in the background are queuing for the 10d, 1/9d and 2/3d. seats. Those were the days! The Empire was demolished in the early 1970's and replaced with the new Grand Junction Hotel, which originally stood in Victoria Street.

Earle Street in the 1950's showing the Market Hall and the Municipal Buildings

Earle Street in the 1950's showing The Mechanics Institute, middle right of picture, the building was demolished in the early 1960's.

Crewe Market Square in the 1950's. Queensway was in its infancy, the Post Office and the Odeon Cinema and its block of shops were still standing. The busses were still using the Square as a terminus, as they had for many years and Delamere Street was still looking like a country lane as the cottages nestled among the trees. But that was about to change as the bulldozers moved in to clear the land for the building of Delamere House and the new buildings replacing the Odeon cinema and the old Post Office.

Goddard Street in the late 1950's, showing the Crewe Locomotive Works entrance and workshops to the right of the picture. The terraced housing has since been replaced by Goddard Court, an old peoples home, and modern housing. The works buildings have also been demolished and the area is now the site of Morrisons Supermarket.

Broad Street in the 1950's, showing the Spring Tavern public house on the corner of Vere Street. That area is now the site of the Beechwood School and its playingfield. While the left of the picture is now occupied by Cypress Court, an old peoples home.

Life went on pretty much as usual while the shops on Queensway were being built in 1954, the clock tower of 'Big Bill' wasn't quite so big when this photograph was taken and the busses were still operating from the square. The man extreme right of the picture is engine driver, Jimmy Hulse.

The houses in Market Terrace have been cleared in readiness for the building of Queensway, which was opened by Queen Elizabeth 11 on the 2nd November 1955. The buildings to the right are the rear of Charles Street and were demolished shortly afterwards. British Homes Stores now stand on the corner to the right of the photograph. This whole area is now pedestrianised.

Queensway in the late 1950's. The Salvation Army Citadel, left of photograph, was bulldozed in 1961. And the Odeon Cinema was demolished in 1983. The area is now pedestrianised.

Work in progress on the M6 Motorway between Sandbach and Middlewich, about 1960. INSET: One of the vehicles used to level the motorway in readiness for its top surface.

The Crewe Bus Station looking in pristine condition not long after its opening in 1960. Crossville double decker busses were taking pride of place when this photograph was taken.

Hightown School being demolished in the 1960s and to the right of that is the Hightown Methodist Church which was demolished around the same time. Kwik Save Garage now occupies the site. To the extreme left of the picture is the St. Paul's Church steeple which was deemed unsafe and pulled down, also in the 1960s.

The Kino Sales Kiosk in the 1960's. This photograph will bring happy memories of 'a night at the pictures' flooding back. The Kino Cinema, which stood in Co-operative Street, was a favourite with many courting couples of the day, not to mention the children who joined the 'tuppenny rush' on a Saturday afternoon. The name of the cinema was later changed to 'The Ritz'. (Inset, top right) Bulldozers demolishing the cinema and Co-operative Street in 1986.

The town centre in the 1960's. By this time busses were using the new bus station and one side of the Market Square had been closed to all traffic. The building to the left centre of the picture (Wildings Ltd) was later demolished and replaced with modern shops. The Adelphi public house, to the right centre, was also pulled down and replaced with shops. This whole area is now pedestrianised. To the left of the picture we see mothers with their large wheeled prams of the day, regal looking when compared with todays buggies!

The junction of Oak Street, Exchange Street, (now Edleston Road), and Wistaston Rd on 15. 6. 1964. To the right, the old Pioneer Anglers Club is being demolished as were the shops on the far side of the road, and in the distance is the Crewe Loco Works Deviation chimney which was pulled down shortly afterwards. This area is now unrecognizable from the way it looked in 1964.

West Street, between Stafford Street and Adelaide Street in 1964. This whole block of buildings was later demolished and is now the site of a garage and its forecourt.

Market Street in 1965. Showing the Adelphi Hotel, to the left of the picture, which was demolish during the redevelopment of the town centre in the late 1960 and 70's, this whole area is now pedestrianised.

The corner of Market Street and Heath Street in the 1970's. These buildings were demolished and the area is now part of the Market centre. The present doors to the market centre would probably feature about centre left in the foreground of this picture.

The Crewe Market
Centre well on the
way to completion
in 1985. The centre
was opened on the
22nd July 1986.

Lockitt Street ready
for demolition in
the 1960's.

Doody's Factory, Nantwich Road, awaiting the bulldozers, is pictured here from Hope Street in 1983.

Looking from The Red Bull entry, across Market Street, and along Earle Street in 1956; the Market Hall and the Municipal Buildings are on the left of the picture.

The passageway between Market Street and Market Terrace; always known as 'The Bull Entry', because of its proximity to the Red Bull public house, left. It was a short cut to Market Terrace, the Salvation Army Citadel, the rear entrance of Woolworths and to the Odeon Cinema; it will also be remembered by many courting couples! The passageway and the Red Bull public house were demolished in the 1960's when huge alterations were made to the centre of the town; making room for the new Market Centre to be built. The Royal Scott public house, on the Middlewich Street Estate, was awarded the Red Bull pub licence.

# THE PEOPLE OF CREWE

A 1940 group of youngsters on a back garden slide in Bedford Street, they will all be in their 70's now. The two ladies in charge are, left Mary and Mrs Brown. From the top of the slide are , Geoff, Ken, Michael, Beryl, Mavis, Doris with doll, Mr Brown and Michael.

Crewe C.W.S. Clothing Factory workers pictured outside the Camm Street Factory in 1912. Note the footwear; all of the girls are wearing clogs!

While barbecues seem to be the in thing these days, picnics were top of the pops in the early part of the 20th century; here we see a group of people enjoying themselves in the 1920's. The teapot and cups seem to be getting lost in the long grass!

A group of Crewe British Legion members pictured before setting out on one of their annual outings in the 1930's. Amongst the group were many of the Crewe Volunteers wearing their South African War Medals and many wearing their first World War decorations.

A Railway Locomotive Works troupe ready to take part in the Crewe Carnival in 1913.

As this proud owner posed with his 1920's car, his little dog pushes in on the picture. I would imagine it will have to grow quite a bit if it wants to see through the car windows while out on a drive!

Three likely lads from the 1920's with their large four door saloon car. In the background we see an advert for Park Drive cigarettes.

A street party in Hulme Street in 1935 to celebrate the silver jubilee of King George V and Queen Mary.

Friends and neighbours of Casson Street, off Ford Lane, celebrating the Silver Jubilee of King George V with this well attended street party in 1935. The lady on the extreme left of the picture is Vera Yoxall with her son Henry.

Children of the Helen Tandy School of Dancing in their Nursery Rhyme Costumes in 1936. The Dancing School headquarters were at the Earl Of Crewe Pavilion on Nantwich Road; they used to present shows at the New Theatre, (now The Lyceum), in Heath Street. The proceeds were donated to the Webb Orphanage.

The last week in June and the first week in July used to herald a mass exodus from the town as Crewe Locomotive Works, the various clothing factories and smaller businesses closed down for the town's wakes weeks. In those days whole families headed for the seaside, and parents, their children, grandchildren and in-laws, would all enjoy a holiday together. Here we see a Crewe family on holiday at Blackpool in 1939.

Elsie Dutton posing for a second world war picture encouraging people to save their food scraps and bones to help the war effort. The photograph was taken on Badger Avenue, Crewe in 1940.

Lady regulars at the Prince of Wales public house on West Street, Crewe, looking forward to their annual fishing match in the 1940's. Here they are posing for a photograph to remember the day, while some of the male drinkers try to push in on the picture! The ladies were residents from Alexandra Street, Naylor Street and Peel Street area which was demolished in the 1960's and 70's. Not all of the names are known, but among those pictured are : Sarah Jones, Annie Blackshaw, Ada Vickers, Mrs Hamlet, Irene Clarke, Sis Sinclair, Violet Greenwood, Mrs L.Readin, Mrs Hulme, Gladys Clarke, Mrs Lawton, Mrs Bossons, Mrs Green, Ernie Vickers and Jimmy Sinclair.

Crewe's 'Dads Army' during the second World War. This Home Guard unit is pictured at their Headquarters at the Crewe Grammar School in 1940. Officers are seated while 'other ranks' stand behind.

Cleaning ladies who worked at the Odeon Cinema in the late 1940's and early 1950's. Not all of their names are known but included in the picture are: Alice Bearpark, Madge Joinson, Ethel Edge and Hilda Francis. The cinema was demolished in 1983.

Crossville bus conductresses, (clippies) at the Queen Street headquarters in 1942. Keeping the girls in order are the two foremen, right and left of picture, also pictured is Miss May McDonald, aged 19 years, fourth from the left, front row. These days she is Mrs May Bebbington.

A West End Street Party celebrating V.E.Day in 1945.

A group of Berkeley Towers employees posing for their photograph during the lunch break in 1947. Included in the picture are Ruby Stead, Marjorie Davies, Betty Barker, Oscar Turner and Helen Clough. (Two names are not known)

Crewe Borough Engineer and Surveyors Department Staff, pictured outside the old fire station in Beech Street East in 1947.

Members of the Crewe Girls Training Corps, in 1947. Their headquarters was at the Bedford Street School. Among those pictured are Pat Elson, Lamela Lindop, Vonda France, Margaret Preston and Beryl Heaton.

Girls Training Corps members pictured in Trafalgar Square on a day out to London in 1947.

Three likely lads, cousins on a day trip to Blackpool in 1948. We didn't own a car, but this side show on the Golden Mile gave us a chance to be photographed in one. Even on holiday, collar and ties were order of the day! Left to right; Ernie Blunstone, Derek Blunstone and yours truly Gordon Davies.

Crewe A.T.C. members proudly pose for a photograph during their summer camp at R.A.F. Rippon in 1950.

Judging by the top coats, it was too cold for a swim, so Yeates Wine Lodge seemed a good bet for these four 'young ladies' on holiday in Blackpool in 1950. Left to right; Hilda Broady, Annie Pennance, Doris Roberts and Renee Edwards.

Employees from the Ministry Of Agriculture, Berkely Towers, Nantwich Road, Crewe taking part in their fancy dress competition on Wednesday 20th December 1950. The first prize went to 'Two little men in a flying saucer', top left of picture.

Milk woman, Betty Cooke, with young Vickey Langley, standing by her delivery van at the Groby Road headquarters of the Kettell's Dairy in 1950.

Members of the Crewe Branch, N.U.R Women's Guild celebrating their diamond jubilee at the Railwaymen's Headquarters in Nantwich Road on 15th February 1958, when over forty sat down to tea, and a jubilee cake was a feature of the table decorations. Among those present were four family members, Mr T.Farrall and Mrs A.Farrall (Secretary), Mrs M.Heathcock (President) and Mrs J.Morris. Also pictured are Len Turnock, Mary Turnock, Mrs Grant, Mr T.Allman, Mr S.William, Mr J.Hughes, Mr S.Heathcock, Mrs M.Allman, Mrs Hughes, Mrs Hurlay, Mrs Williams, Mr C.Robson, Mrs F.Woods (Treasurer), Mrs C.Ruscrow, Mrs Lycott, Mrs E.Orwell (Executive Member), Mrs Hill, Mrs Broomhall, and Mrs H.Jones (National President)

Officers and men of the Crewe Army Cadets in the 1950's.

Officers of the Crewe Army Cadets in the 1950's.

Crewe Pioneer Anglers members pictured on a day trip in the 1950's. The club headquarters were on the corner of Oak Street and Edleston Road until 1962, when they moved to the present address in Underwood Lane.

This charity social evening was held at the Kettell's Hotel in High Street, Crewe in the 1950's. A buffet supper followed by a film show was organised by Mr W.T.Parry, assisted by Mr D.F.Peever, of Messrs Densem's of Market Street, Crewe. Those who attended consisted of managers, proprietors, buyers and shop assistants from the Crewe and Nantwich area.

Staff outside the Hart and Levy Factory, which stood on the corner of Derby Street and Grosvenor Street, in the early 1950's.

Prize winners at a ladies presentation evening at the Engine Public House, Mill Street in the 1950's.

Proud regulars at the Engine Public House, Mill Street, pose with their trophy in this 1950's photograph.

Crewe Air Training Corps members pictured at the Rippon air base while on summer camp in 1950.

Christ Church Rose Queen, Miss J Beech, with her attendants, parading towards the church on 24th June 1953.

Ramsbottom Street residents celebrating the Coronation of Queen Elizabeth 11 in 1953. The venue was the Ramsbotton Street Chapel which was demolished in the 1960's.

More Ramsbottom Street residents waiting to tuck- in at the Coronation party at the Ramsbottom Street Chapel in 1953.

Crewe Sea Cadet Corps leading the 1953 Park Fete down West Street. The building on the left, - at the end of the terraced houses -, has since been demolished and replaced with a Co-op Late- Shop and car park.

Excited youngsters at their Singleton Avenue and Alma Avenue Coronation Party in 1953.

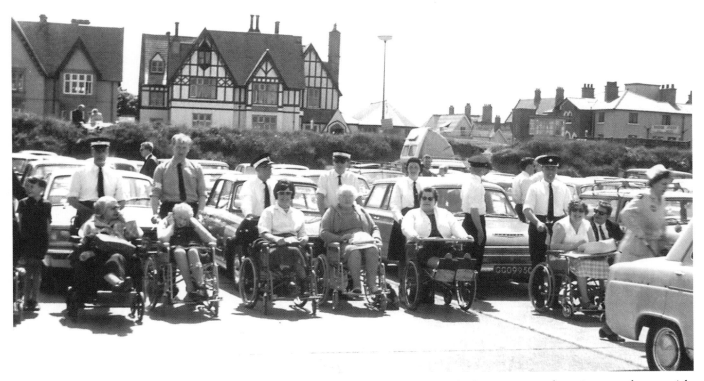

Members of the Crewe St. John Ambulance Division and Crewe Nursing Cadets, are seen here in attendance with patients of the Crewe Orthopedic Clinic after care unit, Nantwich Road, during an annual outing to Rhyl in 1955, which was organised by the Crewe and South Cheshire Motor Club.

Members of the Crewe Blind Welfare Committee enjoying the sunshine during a day trip to Rhyl in 1955, Included in the picture are: Mr Wainwright (President), Mrs Cooke (Secretary), Mrs Gee (Treasurer), Mrs Chesters, Mrs Young and Mrs Bebbington.

Not a very nice day; and dressed against the weather, these children thought the donkey rides were' top of the pops' at the Wheelock Village Fete in the 1960's.

Mothers and toddlers waiting for refreshments at this 1960's Scout Summer Fair.

All the fun of the fair as hopeful youngsters try to win a coconut at this Scout Summer Fair in the 1960's.

Members of the St John's Church Sunday School who took part in the 'Black and White Minstrel Show' at the Church Hall in 1964.

Pensioners enjoying this tuck in at the Hightown Church pensioners party in 1965.

Christine Williams with one of her champion spaniels at the 1965 Crewe Carnival dog show.

More Hightown
Church pensioners
enjoying their
party 1965.

"Our Gang" This artistic picture shows youngsters enjoying themselves in Havelock Street on a dull, February
Sunday morning in 1965. There wasn't much on television in those days, (even if you were lucky enough to own
one). No computers or computer games to occupy the mind, but you can bet these kids never got bored. They
made up their own games, every street was their playground. This area of Mill Street was under demolition at the
time, so it made an ideal site for yet more adventures, Magic! These children will be in their 40's or 50's now, but
hopefully some of them are still living in the Crewe area and will recognise themselves.

Gillian Oldham and Angela Davies enjoying Bonfire night in 1965. Even Shep, the dog, joined in the fun!

Youngsters tucking in at the Crewe Post Office employees childrens Christmas Party in 1968.

A charity fashion show in progress at the Wistaston Memorial Hall in 1968.

More faces at the Crewe Post Office childrens party at the Weston Road headquarters in 1968.

Crowds look on as the Carnival parade passes along West Street in 1970.

The Crewe Carnival progressing along West Street in 1970. On the left hand side of the picture, the old C.W.S. shop and a row of houses had been demolished and the hoarding had been put in place ready for the building of Nova Court, an old peoples residence. To the extreme top right of the picture is The Chetwode Arms, which was built in 1620 and demolished in April 1980 to allow for an extension to West Street; despite protests and demonstrations.

Excited youngsters in Santa's Grotto in 1968.

This happy lot used to be regulars at the old Rifleman public house in Beech Street and are pictured at a reunion at the Rendezvous Club in the 1970's. The Rifleman was pulled down in the early 1960's and the area is now part of the ASDA car park. The Rendezvous Club was above Burton's on Market Street; it went out of business some years ago.

Nylons and tights seem to be the order of the day as these ladies eye-up the bargains on a packed Crewe Market Day in the early 1970's.

Searching for bargains on the old outside market in the early 1970's. The building on the right, formerly an old Chapel, was Lathams the Fruiterers warehouse. It was later demolished along with the buildings in the background, which included a row of shops and the first floor Astoria dancehall.

Local explosives expert, Derek 'Blaster' Bates, presenting Harry Wainwright with his latest L.P. hit 'Laughter with a Bang' . In the early 1970's. Derek was very a popular after dinner speaker. He also toured the theatres with his hilarious one night shows.

A 1960's meeting of the Hospital League of Friends at the old Memorial Hospital, which stood on Victoria Avenue.  Leighton Hospital was opened by Queen Elizabeth on 2nd May 1972.

A well supported
meeting of senior
citizens 1970.

Crewe Sea Cadets parading over Flag Lane Bridge in 1974.

Management staff with their guest, Ken Dodd, at a function they organised for the employees of their pet food company at the Alvaston Hall Hotel in 1976.

Employees and guests watching the star of the show, Ken Dodd entertaining, at the Alvaston Hall Hotel in 1976.

Young fans pose for a photograph with Ken Dodd at the Alvaston Hall Hotel in 1976.

" Who loves ya baby", Mary Smith in an affectionate embrace with her guide dog 'Shandy' in 1976.

Doctor Kay presenting a trophy to members of the Partially Sighted Society, at the Hilary Centre, in 1976.

Pioneer Anglers Club members in good spirits, celebrating the reopening of their premises in Underwood Lane, Crewe, in 1978 after a closure of several weeks while extensive alterations were carried out. The Mayor of Crewe and Nantwich, Councillor Albert Platt cut a ribbon, on stage, in front of over 300 members to officially reopen the premise.

More revellers, having a good time at the reopening of the Pioneer Anglers Club in 1978.

Crewe St.John Ambulance Cadet stand proudly behind their haul of trophies in 1978.

Post Office employees children settle down for their Christmas party at the Post Office Headquarters in Weston Road Crewe in the early 1980's.

Some of the ladies who attended the Rifleman public house reunion at the Redezvous Club in 1980. Norma Barber, Pam Clowes, Christine  ? ,and Win Lewis.

Members of the Crewe St.John Ambulance Cadets pictured at an annual Inspection and Awards evening in 1982.

Two presentations in one in 1982. Here we see Lord Leverhulme presenting the Leverhulme Trophy to Divisional Superintendent, Gwen Davies; and the Cotter Shield to , Member in Charge, Stephen Hodgson of the Crewe Ambulance Cadet Division. County Commissioner, Alan Fielding is to the left of the photograph, while Area Superintendent, Albert Smith is on the right.

Keep it in the family! This group, all related, are pictured at a social evening at the Alvaston Hall Hotel in 1983.

Crewe St John Ambulance Nursing Cadet Division at an enrolment evening at the Municipal Buildings, Earle Street in 1984.

Chronicle kids! These children are pictured enjoying a donkey ride after winning a trip to Blackpool in 1985, courtesy of the Crewe Chronicle.

Ladies of the Crewe Keep Fit squad practicing one of their routines in 1986.

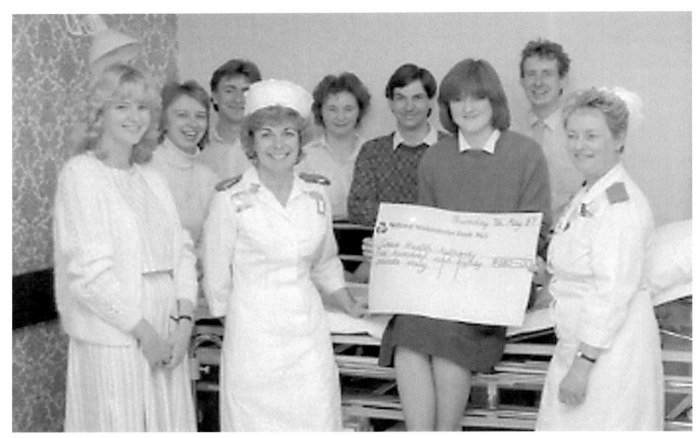

Happy faces at this cheque presentation at the Leighton Hospital in 1987.

Proud parents show of their youngsters after winning in the NORMID 'Mother and Child' competition on 26th October 1987.

Members of the Crewe St John Ambulance Nursing Division with their trophy after coming third in the finals of the Brigade First Aid and Nursing Competitions at the Fairfield Halls, Croydon on the 1st July 1989, when Henry Cooper O.B.E. presented the prizes. Back Row; Henry Cooper O.B.E. Left to Right: Dawn Bowker, Doreen Boardman (Captain) and Kate Machin.

Annie Wigley with relatives and friends on the occasion of her 103rd birthday in 1987. Local M.P. Gweneth Dunwoody, bottom right of picture, also called to wish her a happy birthday!

The team from the Crewe Combined Division which took third place in the St John Ambulance Finals of the First Aid and Nursing Competitions at the Faifield Halls, Croydon on Saturday 1st July 1995. Left to Right: N/M Kate Machin, N/M Dagmar Ball, The RT. Hon. Lord Weatherill D.L. , who presented the trophies and D/O. Doreen Boardman (Captain).

Christmas Revellers at this 1960's party at the Cheshire Cat.

Regulars who used to patronise the Rifleman public house enjoying a reunion evening at the, now defunct, Rendezvous Club, which operated above Burtons shop in the middle of town. The Rifleman was demolished in the 1960's and the area is now part of the ASDA car park.

Included in the picture are: Joe Simmons, Brian Lewis, Colin Barber, Mick Clowes and Johnny Pimlott.

# SPORTING PEOPLE OF CREWE

Three local boxers in the 1920's, the name of the one on the left is not known but Les Hughes, centre, born in 1908, started the first barbell club in Crewe in premises in Ludford Street, later he joined up with Mick Gill and they opened a barbell Club in Hulme Street. Tom Newton, on the right, a well known local boxer in those days, later turned his hand to wrestling when he trained Geoff Condliffe, who wrestled as the famous Count Bartelli. Sadly Tom was killed in January 1971 while returning from a skiing holiday in Austria.

Members of the Crewe Clarion Club proudly group around their trophy after winning a time trial in the 1920's.

Crewe Corinthians posing with their trophies after winning the Haslington Knockout Cup in 1932, following on from successes in the Commander Bailey Cup and the Crewe Memorial Hospital Cup in the same season : Left to right, back row, G.Gibbons, T.Teece, F.Harding, A.Henson, T.Bloss, L.Teece, A.Broughton, and J.Hall.  Front row: R.Teece, C>Graham, F.Dickson, J.Essex, F.Scott, E.Hilditch and P.Furnival (Captain).  Seated on the floor: L.Teece and T.Canty.

Pictured at an exhibition match at the Crewe Golf Club in the late 1930's are professional golfers, second left, Australian Bill Shankland, who played in every British Open from 1937 to 1955; Tony Jacklin was his former assistant; centre is Welshman Dia Reese, and on the right is another Australian, Norman Von Nida. Fred Newton, the late grandfather of David Wheeler, the present Crewe Golf Club professional, is pictured on the extreme left.

Members of the Crewe Barbell Club at their headquarters in Hulme Street in the 1940's. Well known physiotherapist, the late Mick Gill, is pictured second from the right, back row. He later went on to become the Crewe Alexandra physio.

West Street Baptist Church team who won the who were 1st Division Champions of the Crewe Badminton League in 1954-55. Back row; R.Pickstock, B.Hughes, E.Powell and M.Owen. Front; Mrs B.Hughes, Mrs I.Maybury, Mrs F.Farrall and Mrs S.Owen.

The Burton public house domino team with their haul of trophies in 1963.

A presentation evening at the Crewe Alexandra Social Club in the 1960's. Included in the picture are Yvonne Ormes, third from left, Crewe Alex goalkeeper, Willie Mailey and Miss Crewe Alexandra with members and guests.

Lady members of the L.M.R. Social Club, Goddard Street, pictured at their fishing match prize presentation evening in 1961.

A Crewe L.M.R. Cricket team from the 1960's. This picture was taken at the Earle Street Sports Ground, now the site of The Grand Junction Retail Park.

Nantwich Cricket team on their home ground at Whithouse Lane, pictured before taking part in a match in the late 1960's.

Popular local and football league referee, the late Harry Vickers, presenting the referees Good Conduct Cup to the this winning local amateur team in 1965. The trophy is awarded annually by the Crewe and District Referees Society.

Crewe Kings Speedway riders pictured at the Earle Street Sports Ground track in 1969. Left to right: Ken Adams (team manager), Paul O'Neil, Dave Parry, Pete Saunders, Geoff Curtis, Ian Bottomley, Barry Meeks, Maurice Littlechild (Promoter) and sitting on the bike at the front is Colin Tucker. Geoff Curtis, who was probably the Crewe King's biggest star was tragically killed in a track crash in Sydney, Australia, in 1973. Speedway finished in Crewe in 1975; the former sports ground is now the Junction Retail Park.

Two five-a-side football teams pictured before the Carnival Week cup final in the 1970.

Sandbach Ramblers F.C. The new entrants to the Cheshire League took on a selection of Sir Stanley Matthews Port Vale ex-Fourth Division team in a pre-season friendly game in the 1970's.  Sir Stan, playing at centre forward, displayed some of his old tricks before going off at half time. The Sandbach Ramblers team:( including substitutes) : Roberts (Austin), Murphy, Wilson (Ollier), Heald, Webster, Rhodes, Chesworth (Bailey), Barber, Boote, Smith (Carter) and Jenkins. Port Vale ; Sherratt, Boulton, Wilson, James, Chapeman, Miller, Clarke (Coullerton), McClaren, Matthews (Tate), Wilkes (Goodfellow) and Mackenzie. Half of the proceeds went towards the Vale's "Valiant Vale Fund."

The Black Horse football team, photographed on the Crewe Alexandra ground in the early 1970's. The hairstyles and the flared trousers of the guy on the right of the picture make a fashion statement for that period in time. Also, notice the Alex floodlighting in the background!

The Horse Shoe public house football team pictured here on the Crewe Alexandra ground before a cup final against The Black Horse F.C. in the 1970's.

The 1971 Diesel Depot cricket team pictured on the Permanent Way Sports Ground; which, along with the Social Club, has now been closed for several years. Left to right: The late C.Skelling, A.Blunstone, N.Whittingham, C.James, K.Fisher and F.Roberts. Front: B.Smith, the late S.Greatbanks, E.Morris (captain), G.Randell and J.Lowe.

Members of the
Shavington Social
Club Bowls team
pictured in 1973.

And the winners were!
Members of the Ash
Bank Public House Darts
Team who were the "B
Division" Champions of
the Crewe and District
Open League in 1977.
Back row: J.Critchley,
G.Starkey, F.Broomhall,
S.Gaffney, J.Cornes,
J.Appleyard, D.Jennings
and J.Williams. Front
row: P.Newton, A.Jones
(Captain) and A.Broom.

Brian Lewis, is seen here with his array of trophies in 1977. He is holding the Amalgamated Anglers individual trophy; the Challenge Cup, which he won earlier that year, stands on the shelf behind him.

Amalgamated Anglers Club team on their way to take part in the National Fishing finals in 1975.

Winners at the White Lion Weston bowls presentation evening at the Betley Village Hall in the 1980's.

A proud Crewe C.W.S. Football team pose with their trophy in the 1980's.

Past Lady Captains at the Crewe Golf Club pictured at their trophy presentation in 1982 when first place went to Sonia Malins. Pictured are, left to right: Adelaide Cattel, Dora Fisher, Dorothy Morris, Mrs Baker, Anne Newman, Rhonda Leedham, Trudy Brookshaw, Enid Baxter, Mabel Hickman, Sonia Malins, Joan Bishop, Anne Ashworth, Alice Rhead, Ella Duerden, Muriel Boote and Muriel Bradley.

Trophy winners at the 1983 West End Flying Club presentation evening at the Alvaston Hall Hotel.

Crewe F.A. Youth team pictured before a match at the Crewe Alex ground in the 1980's

Trainer Roger Woodward putting Tony Smith and Steve Lloyd through their paces during a training session at the L.M.R. Gymnasium in Richard Moon Street in 1983.

A 1983 Wellcome Foundation F.C squad showing players and officials.

Crewe Grasshoppers Cricket team at the King George Playing Field on 22.7.1984 when they took on Birmingham Ladies C.C. Back row; Hazel Jones, Pam Irving, Julia Wood, Lorraine Maddocks, Linda Cheetham and Kerry Harrop. Front row; Sally Hough, Ann Latham, Liz Arnold Imogene Grosberg and Diane Joyce.

Two Wellcome Foundation cricket teams pictured before their match in 1984.

National Cricket Coach, Imogen Grosberg, founder of the Crewe ladies cricket team 'Grasshoppers' is seen here coaching 10 years old Alison Cutler in 1985. Alison went on to play at junior county level and later for the Cheshire Ladies cricket team, she also played for other representative teams at senior level.

Gerry Davies teeing off on his first day as captain of the Crewe Golf Club in 1989.

Its February 1986, and here we see the 'Crewe Grasshoppers' cricket team lining up for a photograph before a coaching session at the Oakley Centre. Left to right. Ann Latham, Julie Heaton, Diane Goode, Julia Wood, Carol ?, Imogen Grosberg (coach), Alison Cutler and Jenny Crillian. Front row; Julie Crump, Vicki Coates, Diane Joyce and Diane Wakeley.

Local Athlete, Carole Billington who, in 1992 was judged to be the best local athlete, when she won the 'Ann Mackrory Award' and collected £750. In 1993 she was honoured by The Crewe and Nantwich Council when her name was added to the Crewe and Nantwich Borough Sporting Roll Of Honour.

Margaret Adams, watched by her club colleagues, teeing off on the first day as Lady Captain of the Crewe Golf Club in 1989.

# CREWE ALEXANDRA

A Crewe Alexandra team from the beginning of the 20th century. Also pictured are directors and trainers. This photograph was taken outside the old pavilion changing room which stood behind the popular side of the ground.

Enthusiastic Crewe Alexandra fans, complete with their home made 'Robin', at an away match in the 1960's.

Crewe Alexandra Chairman, centre, seated, Norman Rowlinson, Manager Ernie Tagg (to his right) and other Alex directors engaged in a light hearted discussion at the Crewe Alex Club in 1967. Henry Harris, who was the Mayor of Crewe in 1969-70 is seated extreme left of picture. It must have been a 'dry' evening; there isn't a glass in sight!

Popular Crewe Alexandra Player, Gordon Wallace, making a presentation to this five-a-side team in 1968. Gordon made 19 appearances for Liverpool before joining Crewe in 1967. He made a total of 93 appearance for the Alex, scoring 21 goals, before being forced to retire in 1971 because of injuries.

# SCHOOLTIME

Young ladies of the Warmingham Road Church, Sunday School in 1894. Annie Brown, who died at the age of 40 years is on the back row, extreme right.

Girl pupils of the Crewe H.E. School in 1908

An apple for the teacher? I don't think so, in this case it seems to be carrots! Lying on the centre of each desk is a carrot, so we are probably looking in on an art lesson. These youngsters were Borough School pupils in 1912.

Hightown Infants School, 1914. Young Amy Brown, daughter of Annie Brown, featured on the first picture, of this section, is seated on the right hand side of the picture, third row from the front, second from the right.

Pupils of the Haslington C Of E School posing for a class photograph in 1914.

St Mary's R.C. School pupils in 1920 Not all of the names are known but included in the pictured are: Colin Lowndes, Jack Wild, Walter Jones, Harry Wilkinson, Harry Harrison, S.Hulse, Fred Tansey, J.Preece, Jeff Hulse, Vera Yoxall, Mary Taylor, Dott Pilling, Elizabath Emmett, Minnie Hodgass, Mary High and Ilene Durkin.

These boy pupils from the West Street School opted to have some of their toys with them when they posed for this photograph in the early 1920's, including two horses and a dray at the front of the picture.

West Street School Pupils in the mid 1920's. The school was later demolished to make way for a new road junction.

Class of 1922 at the Hightown School. These young ladies were in group 6. Amy Brown, mentioned in the previous photographs is second from the left on the back row. She had four daughters of her own; she died in 1995 at the age of 86 years. As the name suggests, Hightown School stood in Hightown; was demolished some years ago and is now the site of the Kwik-fit Garage.

Staff members and pupils at the Adelaide Street Boys School in 1928. Not all of the names are known, but included on the pictured are: Headmaster Mr Tom Bamford, left, the other teacher is Mr Powell. Pupils, Raymond Poole, Eric Burgess, John Cope, Stan Treywin, Doug Campbell, Joe Slack, Doug Parker, Ernie Cope, Wilf Vicker and Jack Maybury (sitting third from the headmaster on the second row) who, in later life, went on to become the Crewe and Nantwich Sports Council Chairman.

How's this for a risky gym lesson? A boy leaping from a bar chair, over a rope, held by two of his class mates; his posture is like a pair of braces as he flies through the air. I don't think it would be allowed in this day and age! This was a physical training exercise at the old Borough School in 1940.

An Adelaide Street School football team from the 1940's  Back row: B.Whennan, C.Prophet, B.Ackerly, R. Goyer, H.Gill, J.Ecleston. Kneeling; Atkin, R.Brereton, T.Mooney, G.Potts and F.Robinson.

Brierley Street pupils with their teacher, Mr Oxenbald, pictured during a visit to a local farm in 1948.

Young Brierley Street School pupils with their collection of flowers an leaves while on a nature walk in 1948.

A Brierley Street School Photograph in the school yard in 1948. In the background is the old senior school which is now a business centre.

Budding artists hard at work in Miss Smith's art class in 1949.

Boys will be boys! These young Brierley Street School pupils are digging the soil from a rabbit's burrow, during their school visit to a farm, while the young lady keeps her distance.

Playtime with a Hoola-hoop at the Brierley Street School in 1949.

Brierley Street School teaching staff in 1950. Back row; Mr Oxenbald, Not Known, Mr Tyson, Not Known, Miss Brenchley, Mrs Cornes, Mrs Hasledine, Not Known and Miss Clarke.

Young Brierley Street School pupils with young Christmas trees in 1950.

More Brierley Street Primary School pupils in fancy dress in readiness for their school play in 1950. Among those pictured are; J.Curley, D.Roberts, D.Lewis, J. Jones, P Smith, P Palin, D Wright and B Elliott.

Brierley Street
Football team,
1950-1 season,
pictured with
teachers Mr
Oxenbald and
Mrs Haseldine.

Brierley Street School pupils line up for a picture in the 1950's.

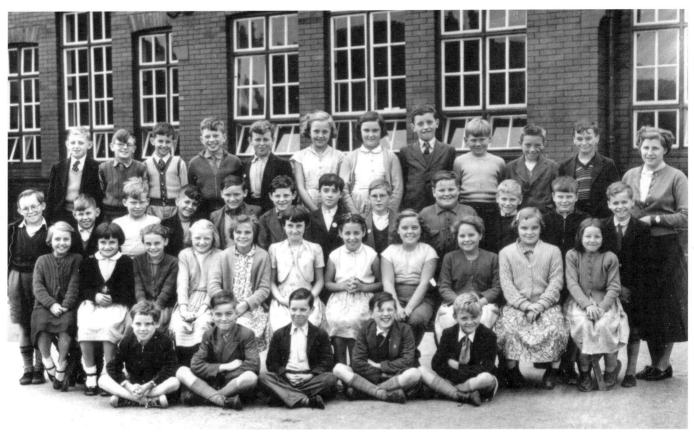

Brierley Street School Junior pupils in the 1950's.

Brierley Street Junior School Pupils in the 1950's.

Brierley Street Junior School pupils 1950's.

Brierley Street School Junior pupils in the 1950's.

Brierley Street School Junior School pupils 1950's.

This is a Brierley Street Junior football team from the early 1950's, pictured on the Middlewich Street Playing Fields. Their boots look very heavy, with nailed on studs, and those toe caps look as if they could do quite a lot of damage during a match.

Smile please! Broad Street Primary School Pupils pose for their school photo in 1951.

Children posing for a photograph when one of the many sheep tries to get in on the act! These pupils from the Mill Street Primary School were enjoying an outing to the Horseshoe Pass, Llangollen in 1953. Among those pictured are: Elva Davies, Joan Chapman, Vivian Wright, Brian Beech, Harry Armstrong, Norma Crogan, Gillian Chetta, Kay Ellis, Heather Donovan and John Davies.

Edleston Road School pupils pose for this Coronation year photograph in 1953.

Mill Street Primary School pupils enjoying a day trip to London in 1955. Here they are pictured on the steps of St Pauls Cathedral with their teacher Mr Jervis, to the right of the back row.

Bedford Street Senior Girls School Choir in 1955, with teachers Mrs Palmer and Miss Ellis in attendance.

Ludford Street School Senior Boys pupils in 1955. Among those pictured are Robert Cartwright, Alan Lewis, Moggy Gibbons, Duncan Parker and Freddy Telford.

This is the Adelaide Street School Choir of 1956 when they took part in a choir festival at the Crewe Grammar School, Ruskin Road. Back row: Mr Geaorge Durber (Headmaster), Miss Boughy, Jackie Lowndes, Not Known, Susan Latham, Miss K.Brooke. Second row: Colin Prophet, Shirley Henshall, Not Known, Jeanette Gilchrist, Margaret Johnson, Moira Parrot, Not Known, Susan Blakemore, Elizabeth Smith, Not Known, Jaquline Keeling and Pamela Roberts. Third Row. Barbara Deakin, Margaret Broady, Not Known, Christine Farrrell, Pat French, Wendy Davies, Bernice Boulton, Pat Baker, Christine Lloyd and Pat Preston. Front row: Not Known, Not Known, David Edwards, Frank Robinson, Barry Lapping, Not Known, Not Known, and Not Known.

Ludford Street Boys School Swimming team in 1956. Pictured are; H.Williams, C.Hand, R. Mason, Ronald Porteous, A.Payne, D.Wells, Brian Jones, Alan Maybury, C.Glassey, D.Boddington and J.Perkins.

Kings Grove School senior girl pupils in the late 1960's

A Wistaston Green Junior School football team from the 1960's

With the table laid in readiness for their 1960's Christmas party, these youngsters are finding it difficult keep their mind on the school carol singing.

Pensive pupils gathered at their prize giving day at the Ludford Street School in 1962.

West Street Junior School pupils photographed in 1964. The school later became a Crewe Works canteen but was later demolished to make way for the West Street road junction leading to the Morrison's store.

Crewe Alexandra goalkeeper, Willie Mailey, presenting the Impact Cup to an excited Ludford Street Junior team in 1965.

Brierley Street Junior Girls School pupils with their teachers in 1965.

Two junior school football teams pose with the Timperley Shield before this game in 1965.

Ludford Street Boys School Senior football team in 1965.

Wistaston School girls netball team receiving their trophy from the Mayoress of Crewe, Mrs H.P. Vernon after an interschool competition in 1966.

A group of staff and students at the British Railways Training Centre, Webb House, Victoria Avenue, in 1966.

Ludford Street Boys School junior football team showing off their shield after a successful season in 1966.

A line up of the Ludford Street School teaching staff in 1966.

Prizewinners at the Ludford Street Girls School in 1967. Carol Marvel is seated on the left of the front row.

The victorious Ludford Street School football team pictured at the Crewe Alexandra ground in 1967 when they won the Bill Houston Knock-out Cup. Unfortunately, Les Wain, the captain, extreme right, had been injured in a previous match and had to sit this one out.

A large cast of pupils rehearsing for their school play in the early 1970's.

Coppenhall School pupils proudly showing some of their work while in preparing for a parents evening in 1967.

Trainee Chefs at work in the South Cheshire College kitchen. Head of the department is Neil Ramshaw, left of picture.

A Ludford Street Boy's School badminton team in 1967.

Members of the Ludford Street School Badminton team in 1967.

A meeting of former pupils at the Crewe Grammar School, Ruskin Road, in 1970.

Students at work in the College Restaurant in 1968. On this occasion, College Principal George Moore, second from the left, sits down to a meal with friends. The restaurant is open on a daily basis to college visitors.

Pupils at the Kingsway School await their turn as one brave soul shows them how to summersault in 1969. Meanwhile sports teacher, Mr Monkhouse keeps a watchful eye on the action during this trampoline lesson.

How best to cook the Sunday Roast. Head of department, Neil Ramshaw, holds the pan as a this student examines the roasting meat.

Pupils and staff at The Crewe County Grammar School For Girls in 1977. Photo 1.

Pupils and staff at The Crewe County Grammar School for Girls in 1977. Photo 2.

Pupils and staff at the Crewe County Grammar School for Girls in 1977. Photo 3.

Pupils and staff at the Crewe County Grammar School in 1977. Photo 4.

Pupils and staff at The Crewe County Grammar School in 1977.

A 1980's Kings Grove School Badminton Team. Back Row ; Chris Raisewell, Mattew Barley, Mrs Howell, John Corbett and ? Dutton. Front row: Lyndon Hall, Craig Welsh, Daryl Williams and Darren Owen.

This is how the school photographs were produced in the days of the old Borough School. Children were sat down in lines against an old sheet. The photographs would then be cut to individual portraits.

Kings Grove prefects in the early 1980's: Matthew Moss, Laura Harding, Craig Wakefield, Charlotte Smedley and Natalie Street.

Kings Grove School pupils enjoying a day trip away from school their school work in the early 1980's.

Kings Grove High School pupils taking part in a school play in the 1980's

Brierley Street School Headmaster Mr Jones is almost lost in a sea of faces in the centre of this 1980's photograph.

Ship-a-hoy! These youngsters from the Brierley Street School are pictured during a school play in the early 1980's.

Ludford Street School Headmistress, Miss McIntyre, accompanying Princess Margaret as she meets the pupils during a visit to the school in 1981. The pupils, left to right are: Bernard Felton, Lisa Gowans, Julie Davies, Anita Smith, Stephanie Peevers, Andria Coyles, Elizabeth ? , Lynda Latham and Michelle Birtles.

Beechwood C.J.School pupils pose with their trophy after winning the local schools Cup competition in 1982. Back Row: I.Williams, S.Smith, G.McCulloch, C.Moyle, S. Griffiths, R.Cooper, P.Leslie. Front Row: R.Singh, L.Bickerton, N.Butterworth, H.Owen (Captain), M.Broome, J.Fairlamb and C.Heath.

Mums, Helpers and toddlers at the Broad Street School Playgroup Christmas party in 1983.

Gainsborough Junior School football team pose for a team photograph in 1986.

Kings Grove School football team which won the Crewe School's Fourth Year football knock-out in 1983-84. Among those pictured are: Teacher Ian Cowap, Graham Packer, Chris Johnson, Richard Farrington, Mark Kendal, Kevin Madeley, Craig Baldini, David Dale, Andrew Newton, Stephen Tew, Neil Watson and Paul Tomkinson.

Kings Grove School netball players of yesteryear who won the South Cheshire Schools' league and tournament in 1984. Featured are Jenny Grocott, Nicole Ankers, Mandy Wainwright, Alison Jennings, Lisa Smith, Karen Aylward, Tracey Keaveney, Salma Sadler, Donna Hand, Nicola Oxborough, Angala O'Neal, Sarah Moulton and Rachel Tomkinson.

The Crewe Schools junior football team, pictured at the Gainsborough Road playing field in 1986.

Young members of the Yvonne School of Dancing, pictured here in 1988.

More Dancers at the Yvonne School of Dancing in 1988.

Kings Grove School pupils in holiday mood in 1989.

Kings Grove pupils in period costume Left to right, standing: Sean Carter, Michael Betts, Damien Pye, Mark Pearl and Paul Tomkinson. Seated: Clare Manley, Rebecca Leech, Stacey ? and Joanne Scragg.

Winning Victoria High School pupils with their Music Festival trophies in 1986.

Kings Grove School assembly photograph in 1981.

# ROLLS ROYCE
## Rolls-Royce and its Crewe Beginnings

TUESDAY 5TH JULY 1938 began as just another day down on Merrill's Farm. The serried ridges of the potato fields were in full flower. Nearby, cattle grazed contentedly, just as they had for as long as anyone could remember on this rural corner of Crewe. But before the day was over, urgent instructions from the Crewe Town Hall arrived to disrupt the farm managers' routine.

WEDNESDAY 6th July 1938 was altogether different. The cows had been herded to pastures new, never to return. The potatoes would surely be swept aside during the onslought that had just begun, for a convoy of earth-moving machines had trundled along Pym's Lane and were now stripping the topsoil. This was Crewe's biggest construction project since the railway works were built here some sixty years earlier and was well under way.

The arrival of the bulldozers came after weeks of speculation. Three months earlier, Rolls-Royce and the Air Ministry had started searching for a site, far away from the company's main plant at Derby, on which to erect a factory to make aero engines for the Royal Air Force.

The Government wanted Rolls-Royce to create extra capacity so that the engine output could be increased still further - and very rapidly - in the event of a war with Germany.

On May 24th the Air Ministry had decided that the factory would be built at Crewe. Those in the know regarded it as the best news Crewe had had for years: 2,315 people in the district were unemployed or working short time, out of a total of 46,000. New jobs were needed desperately.

On the 14th of June, surveyors were sent to Merrill's Farm to peg out the outline of the factory. A week later Rolls-Royce Limited's General Works Manager, Ernest Hines, told the Crewe Chronicle, "We shall be very disappointed if we have not got the factory in production by Christmas". Three hundred men would be recruited immediately but eventually several thousand would be needed.

Hines statement lifted the gloom that had settled over Crewe during many years of depression, caused by the loss of 4,000 jobs at the railway works since the First World War.

Thanks to Rolls-Royce the future was suddenly brighter. Few, in Crewe, gave much thought to the fact that the promise of prosperity stemmed from the threat of another war.

Rolls-Royce had narrowed its choice of sites to two - one in Weston Lane (now Weston Road), the other at the Merrill's Farm, which proved to be 'very desirable' - about sixty acres of reasonably level ground, offered by the Crewe Corporation for £104 an acre, with good access from Pym's Lane, which had recently been widened and was due to join a main road some 500 yards away, the Middlewich Road. The Corporation also assured that the electricity, gas, water and drainage services could easily be connected to the site: houses for the factory workforce could be built nearby.

On day eight Hines and the Air Ministry Officials had final discussions with the Crewe Corporation. Two weeks later the

Early days at the Rolls-Royce Factory in Pyms Lane, Crewe, in 1940.

Ministry formally sanctioned £1 million to finance the first phase of the factory and an additional aero plant at Derby. On that day the Rolls-Royce factory made its first mark on Crewe in the form of pegs driven into the turf at the Merrill's Farm.

Merrill's Farm was laid bare and steel for the factory's building frames arrived. By the end of July the first structure - No1 Stanchion, at the North West corner of the Main Shop - was erected.

By mid-September the framework for most of the shop's 35 bays, each 240ft wide by 30ft long had been assembled. The weather was atrocious. The site became a sea of mud and a sleeper road had to be laid so that building materials could be delivered.

As the builders laboured to clad the skeleton before the winter set in, Crewe's recruits could at last gain a proper impression of the place where they would soon be working round-the-clock to dispatch Merlins to the Royal Air Force.

The installation of Machinery proceeded bay-by-bay, as soon as the concrete floors hardened. There was a timber screen across the open end of the factory. As each bay was completed the screen was moved back and more machines were brought in.

By the 18th of October 1938, the roofs and walls of the Main Shop were completed, a partition capable of keeping out the winter weather was near bay 11 and the factory began making aeroengine parts. In the months that followed work progressed on the ancillary buildings - engine test beds, laboratories and the heat treatment shop, including the office block facing Pym's Lane.

Crewe's first Merlin engine, a Merlin 11, was completed on 20th May 1939. This was day 361 of the Crewe project; only 45 weeks had passed since the bulldozers started leveling Merrill's Farm. During the next few days the engine was run at full throttle and despite a 20ft wall and a series of silencers to deflect the noise, the row could be heard for miles around. The engine passed its test and was dispatched on the 10th of June. Thousands more followed. From the outset it was known that

the Main Shop and its ancillary buildings would merely be the nucleus of a vast factory.

The Air Ministry authorized the first two phases of the expansion which, by 1943, would enable the number of employees at the factory to peak at 9,878 and annual output surge from 208 engines in 1939 to 6,085.

Britain's Air Minister, Sir Kingsley Wood, attended celebrations marking the first anniversary of the commencement of construction at Crewe.

Over the next five years many VIP's visited the factory including King George V1 and Queen Elizabeth, fighter and bomber pilots (who thanked the workers for their efforts) and also Jack Payne, Henry Hall and Wilfred Pickles, who entertained them in the canteen and ballroom, which opened in 1940.

Seven weeks after Sir Kingsley's visit, Britain was at war. By this time the factory had its own Home Guard Unit (The Seventh Cheshire) and a cordon of pillboxes, barrage balloons and artillery.

Joiners built a model factory in the ballroom, camouflage experts climbed stepladders to squint at it from all angles through the wrong end of binoculars. From these antics emerged a camouflage scheme which made the factory hard to spot from the air. Nevertheless, on December 29th 1940 a JU 88 German bomber saw through the disguise. Two of its bombs hit the factory - one destroying a sub-station, the other hitting part of the second machine shop. Fortunately it was the only occasion came under attack.

After the war ended in 1945 the factory was converted to build motor cars. The car that had the distinction of becoming the first post-war model, Crewe's first car, and the first car ever built by the company, was not a Rolls-Royce at all - it was a Bentley MK V1, derived from the Rolls-Royce Wraith of 1938/39. The first post-war Rolls-Royce was the Silver Wraith, introduced in 1947.

A well attended Rolls-Royce dinner in the 1940's. Not all of the names are known but included in the picture are Ron Dyson, Geoff Blaston, Vaughn Lewis, Wilson Elliott, Harold Peake and N.Wiggett.

Welfare Manager, Mr Hunstone, (left of picture) arranging the children of Rolls- Royce employees in readiness for a march to the sports field to take part in the 1947 Field Day.

Employees children are loaded onto wagons and the parade moves away from the factory, proceeding to the Rolls-Royce field for the annual sports and field day in 1950.

A 1950's Rolls- Royce cricket team. Not all of the names are known but included in the photograph are; Wilson Elliott, Eric Jones, Jack Prince, Jack Amos, J Bickerton, Charlie Tagg, Ernest Buchan and Joey Dixon

This photograph from the 1950's was sent from Australia by Harold Smith, fourth from the right, who emigrated to Victoria many years ago. Here he is pictured with his Rolls-Royce colleagues, outside the Boiler House before leaving for the sunshine. Harold and his wife Margery are now living in a retirement village, where, he has been President of the Senior Citizens Club for eight years. The proud couple now have eleven great grand children.

A Rolls- Royce cricket team from the 1950's, left to right, back row: Tim Byrms, J.Hewitson, Jack Cotton, E.Poynton, Bill Bailey, Len Ord (groundsman), Unknown, Wilson Elliott and Bill Elliott. G.Walker, E.Jones, J.Knight, J.Prince, E.Buchan and J.Amos.

This was a well attended Saturday Dance Night at the Rolls- Royce Starlight Room in 1955.

This little girl proudly collects her prize at a 1958 Rolls- Royce Field Day. Also pictured are Wilson Elliott (seated left), Jack Valentine (Standing), Elsie Valentine and Barbara Fishburne (seated) while Mrs E.Stafford is looking at the prizes.

Lord and Lady Hines, centre, thanking management and staff after a camera and a sewing machine had been presented to them during a visit to the factory in 1958.

Popular Jack Valentine enjoying the company of three pretty ladies at his retirement party which was held at the Rolls- Royce Starlight room in 1960.

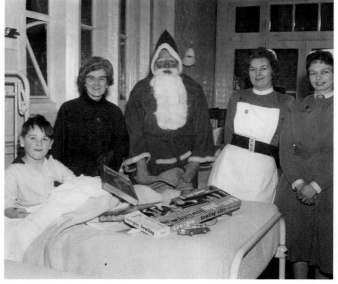

The Rolls - Royce Works Managers wife, Mrs Elsie Stafford, seen here spreading Christmas cheer when she visited the children's ward, at the Crewe Memorial Hospital in the 1960's. Also pictured are the ward sister and nurse and of course, Father Christmas. The Memorial Hospital, which stood on Victoria Avenue, was replaced by Leighton Hospital which opened on 2nd May 1972 by Queen Elizabeth 11.

Head of department, Arthur Gilbert, to the left of the table, pictured with staff and colleagues at his retirement presentation at the Roll-Royce factory in 1965.

Mr George Eardley, winner of the Victoria Cross and Military Medal in 1944, pictured on the occasion of his retirement from Roll-Royce on the 26th February 1971. Here we see Plant Equipment Engineer Manager, Wilson Elliott, presenting Mr Eardley with a cheque. Also pictured are, Sid Torr, second from right, Mr Neville and Mr P.Rose who is to the left of photograph.

Rolls-Royce employees having a great time at the Rolls-Royce Club, celebrating the retirement of their colleague, Fred Hulse, in 1972. Left to right, front row: Mrs Hulse, Fred Hulse, two of their Nantwich friends, Bertha Thompson, Joan Elliott, Jean Rose, and Mrs Prangley. Bach row, left to right: Len Thomson, Wilson Elliott, Jack Norton, Charles North, Walter Jones, Sid Torr, Tom Gardner and Peter Rose.

Rolls - Royce Badminton team 1976.

Wilson Elliott ( holding his retirement gift), at his retirement presentation in the Rolls Royce Starlight Room on 19th January 1978. Also pictured are his work colleagues.

Some of the retired Rolls- Royce employees pictured before two coach loads left for a trip to the seaside in 1979.

Santa and his helpers give assurance to these slightly bewildered youngsters as they posed for a seasonal photograph at the Rolls-Royce starlight room in 1987.

Employees line-up to welcome Her Majesty Queen Elizabeth 11 during her visit to the Rolls-Royce factory in 1987

It was a real blow to the Crewe Rolls-Royce Factory football team to learn that after winning their way through to the finals of two knock-out competitions in 1976, they would have to play both games on the same evening! Nevertheless on Friday, 21st may that year they fielded two sides and though a goalkeeper was played in attack and several old hands were brought out of retirement, both teams turned in outstanding performances. One team beat Crewe Red Star, 4-1, to win the Commander Bailey Cup for the second year running, and the other team, although dominating the final of the Sandbach Ramblers Knockout Competition, lost to a late goal from the Wheelock X1 in the closing minutes of the match. Here we see both teams celebrating their mixed fortunes in the Sports and Social Clubs Valantine Pavilion.

# MAYORAL OCCASIONS

Flying at Crewe in 1921. This photograph was taken at Merrills Farm, Rolls Bentley Factory now stands on the land. Among the guests was the Mayor of Crewe, Councillor Rupert Darlington.

The Mayor and Mayoress of Crewe, Councillor and Mrs Booth pictured at the South Cheshire Badminton finals when they presented the trophies in 1956.

Local dignitaries and their wives pictured with the Nantwich Chairman, Dora B.Bowen, third from the left,seated, at the Chairman's Ball on the 17th December 1956. Also on the picture is the Crewe Mayor G.E.Hodkinson E.S.Q.

This picture was taken on the 28th April 1959 at a senior citizens party at the Wedgewood Church Hall, which was in Heath Street. The Mayor and Mayoress of Crewe, Councillor and Mrs Tom Consterdine were in attendance. On the back wall is a poster advertising the wrestling at the Crewe Town Hall, a popular local sport in those days.

In 1965 a competition was organised to raise money for the St John Ambulance Headquarters in Bedford Street, Crewe. A watch was locked away for a period of time and people were invited to guess at which time the watch would stop. Here we see the watch being handed over to the Mayor of Crewe, Councillor J.O.Hughes, for secure keeping in the mayoral safe. Pictured left to right are; Joan Waring, Albert Smith, Mayor, J.O.Hughes, Arthur Capper and Dorothy Yates. Standing in the background are nursing members and nursing cadets.

These ladies were queuing hoping to win a tombola prize at the Mayor's Ball in 1965. The tickets were only one shilling each and the proceeds would help to swell the funds of Mayor J.O.Hughes's charity.

The Mayoress of Crewe, Mrs H.P.Vernon, sixth from the left, pictured with Inner Wheel officials at a luncheon in 1966.

The Ritz Cinema Manager, Mr Williams, left of picture, welcoming the Mayor and Mayoress of Crewe, Councillor and Mrs H.P.Vernon, accompanied by Crewe Councillors, to a late night viewing of the film "Women In Love" in 1966. The Ritz, formerly the Kino Cinema, was demolished in 1986.

This was Armistice Sunday, November 1966, on the Crewe Market Square when local organisations gathered in front of the War Memorial. Two representatives wait to lay their wreathes, while the mayor's Chauffeur and mace bearer, Maurice Howell, stands in front of the civic party which includes the Mayor of Crewe, Councillor H.P. Vernon.

The Mayor of Crewe, Councillor H.P. Vernon, minus his chain of office on this occasion, was surrounded by the machinists, who were offering advice when he tried his hand at working a sewing machine during a visit to this local factory in 1966.

The Mayor of Crewe, Councillor Herbert Vernon, receiving the Queen's Award For Industry on behalf of the Crewe Borough, in 1966.  Councillor Syd Bayman is standing second from the right of the picture.

Rotary Club members pictured at the Lamb Hotel, Nantwich. Their guest for the evening was the 1966-67 Mayor of Crewe, Councillor H.P.Vernon (Centre front).

The Mayor and Mayoress of Crewe, Councillor and Mrs H.P.Vernon, pictured with their family in the mayors parlour, immediately after the mayor making in 1966.

The Mayor and Mayoress of Crewe, Councillor and Mrs Herbert Vernon (seated right), entertaining guests in the mayor's parlour in 1967. Councillor and Mrs Don Holt are seated left.

The 1966-7 Mayoress of the Crewe Borough, Mrs H.P. Vernon, crowning the Carnival Queen as her attendants look on.

It was all smiles for the Mayor and Mayoress, Councillor and Mrs Wilf Talbot, when they paid a surprise visit to this childrens party in 1968.

The Mayor of Crewe, Councillor H.P.Vernon, presenting budding artists with their prizes after their success in a painting competition organised by the Crewe Borough Council in 1967.

The 1967-68 Mayor of Crewe, Councillor Frank Holme, receiving a gift from the railway company during his visit to the Railway Works General Offices in Market Street, Crewe. Works Manager, Mr Frank De Nobrega is in the centre of the group.

The Mayor and Mayoress of Crewe, Councillor and Mrs Wilf Talbot, pose for a photograph with the ladies of the Crewe Business and professional Ladies Club before their annual dinner at the Crewe Arms Hotel on 19th September 1968. The Mayoress, Sheila Talbot, is seated in the centre of the front row.

The Mayor of Crewe, Councillor Henry Harris making a presentation to local G.P. Doctor E. Clulow, a member of the Railway Museum Committee, in 1969.

Council Officer, Malcolm Elliott, receiving a gift from the Mayor of Crewe and Nantwich, Councillor Peter Kent, on the occasion of his retirement in 1985. Looking on are Mayoress, Marie Kent, Mr Elliott's wife, Vera and his mother Kathleen.

The Mayor of Crewe and Nantwich, Councillor Les Wood receiving a Life Line presentation from students of the South Cheshire College in 1986. Project Manager Roger Slinn is to the left of the picture.

The Wistaston Brownies were all smiles when they were guests of the Mayor and Mayoress of Crewe and Nantwich, Councillor and Mrs Les Wood, during a visit to the Mayors reception room in 1986.

The Mayor of Crewe and Nantwich, Councillor Les Wood, with students and staff members of the South Cheshire College of Further Education, after a presentation ceremony at the mayors reception room in the Municipal Buildings, Earle Street in 1986.

The Mayor and Mayoress of Crewe and Nantwich, Councillor and Mrs Les Wood, pictured with a group of pensioners from the Wellcome Foundation, during a visit to The Mayor's Parlour and Council Chamber in 1986.

The Mayor and Mayoress of Crewe and Nantwich, Councillor and Mrs Alan Pheasey were in attendance to present the certificates to these youngsters at the North West Road Safety Group meeting in 1990.

Retiring Mayor Alice Roberts, handing over the chain of office to the new Mayor, Leonard Turnock, in May 1989. Mayoress Mrs Turnock is to the right.

The Mayor and Mayoress of Crewe vond Nantwich, Councillor and Mrs Richard Ellwood, ( sitting on each end of the middle row), pictured with the St John Ambulance Officers and Nursing Cadets at a presentation evening at the Municipal Buildings, after the cadets won the Cotter Shield in 1994.

Take Three Mayors.........the 1966-67 Mayor of Crewe Councillor H.P. Vernon, left of centre, is pictured shaking hands with his successor, Councillor Frank Holme, 1967-68. Also pictured is Deputy Mayor, Donald Holt who became Mayor of the Crewe Borough in 1973-74. In fact he was the last Mayor of the old Crewe Borough before incorporation, when it became "The Borough of Crewe and Nantwich District Council". Their wives are looking on.

The Mayor and Mayoress of Crewe and Nantwich, Councillor and Mrs John Bedson, look on as Coronation Street star Gerry Booth (the late Graham Haberfield) cuts the ribbon to officially open Ringways Garage, which stood on the corner of Samuel Street and Hightown; the business later moved to Macon Way. Councillor John Bedson was the first Mayor of the newly formed Borough of Crewe and Nantwich District Council in 1974. Town Clerk, Alan Brook and his wife, Marjorie, are pictured second and third from the left of the picture.

# RAILWAY LEGACY

The "Ionie" steam engine with its seven coaches pictured during its non-stop run from Carlisle to London on September 8th 1895. At an average speed of 55 miles per hour.

Grandparents, parents and children pose for a picture at the Elton, Sandbach, level crossing in this early 20th century picture.

46244 King George V1. A ' Princess Coronation' Class 7P engine designed by Sir William Stanier in 1937. Originally a streamlined locomotive it is pictured here, after being converted, outside the Crewe Works Paint Shop in 1947, wearing the new British Rail colours. The area where this engine is standing is now the site of the Morrisons supermarket.

The 1939 Crewe Carnival Queen and her attendants pictured here with Erecting Shop staff during a guided tour of the Crewe Locomotive Works.

The 1939 Carnival Queen and her two attendants, seen here in the Crewe Works Erecting shop, are studying a repair to the cowling of a streamlined steam engine, while the young apprentices seem to be more interested in studying the girls!

Crewe Works Machine Shop employees on a day trip in the 1940's.

Proudly posing for a photograph on 'one they'd made earlier' are this gang of fitters in the Crewe Works Erecting Shop in the 1940's.

A Crewe Locomotive Works football team showing off their trophy after a Cup Final on the Goddard Street ground in the 1940's.

While their men were away at the war, these ladies contributed to the war effort in the Crewe Locomotive Works, working on lathes, machines and untold numbers of other jobs. Hilda Tudor, pictured here third from the right on the back row, worked one of the giant overhead cranes in the Erecting Shop.

In 1949, after performing to a sell-out crowd at the Plaza Cinema in High Street, on the previous evening, 'song bird' Petula Clark is seen here on a guided tour of the Crewe Works. During her walk-about, she stopped for a chat with machinist, Peggy Lowe (nee Brookhouse), Peggy was one of the many wartime women workers who played an important role in the war effort and immediate post-war years. Petula later featured in the long-running television series THE HUGGETS which starred Jack Warner, who was perhaps better remembered as P.C. George Dixon in the series, DIXON OF DOCK GREEN.

A quiet
Sandbach
Station,
Elworth, in
the 1940's.

A Black 5 engine
leaving the
Basford Hall
Marshalling
Yard, in the
1950's, with its
heavy load.

Some of the Crewe North Shed cyclists, and their supporters, who took part in the annual five miles cycle race, around the old park, in 1952.

The breakdown gang from the North Shed Motive Power Section, Crewe, who attended the Harrow and Wieldstone crash in 1952.

A British Railways, Class 2, 2-6-2 Mixed Traffic Tank Locomotive pictured during assembly at the Crewe Works Erecting Shop in 1954.

Fitters and fitters mates from the Crewe North Engine Shed, celebrate their pools win in 1958. The second dividend netted them £800 each. Left to right; F.Bratherton, F.Carr, George Randell, G.Oliver, L.Tuppin, Mrs L.Potts, Roy Francis and Walley Potts.

Employees from the Railway General Offices, Chester Bridge, pictured at their annual staff party at the Crewe Arms Hotel in November 1960.

Drivers and firemen (Sheddies) from the Crewe North Locomotive Shed pictured during a day trip to Blackpool in the early 1960's. Top of the bill on the North Pier that year were Joan Regan and the King Brothers.

Quiet as the grave, in Crewe Works. These steam engines are awaiting the cutters torch as the steam era draws to a close in the 1960's.

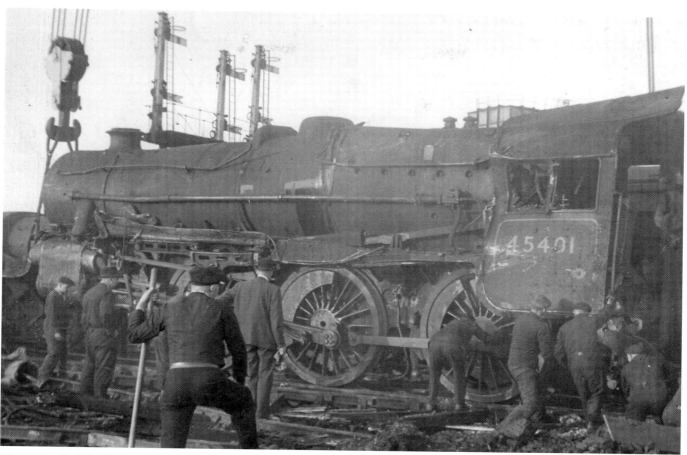

Team work. The Crewe breakdown gang swarm around this engine, to make it safe, as the giant crane lifts it upright after a collision with a passing train on August 28th 1961.

Roof maintenance joiners repairing a roof in the Old Works section of the Crewe Loco Works in 1962.

'It's a hard life!' Crewe Works Joiners Shop Staff enjoying a break in 1962.

British Rail employees having a great time in Austria in 1963. The holiday was organised by British Rail and the total cost for travel, the hotel and full board was just £16 per person! Bring back the good old days!

A gang of Crewe Locomotive Works joiners repairing a workshop roof in 1963.

Geoff Oliver, left, and John Lowe, working on engine 6100, Royal Scot, at the Crewe North Engine Shed, in 1964. Edley Hulse is looking down from the footplate.

Just the ticket! Staff at the British Railways Ticket Printing Factory, which was situated in Bridle Road, hard at work in 1965.

Engine Driver Tom Blakemore at the controls of an Electric train standing in Crewe Station in 1965. Tom Started Work at the Crewe North Engine Shed in 1934, as an engine cleaner. He progressed to the footplate, becoming a fireman on the main line trains. After many years he was promoted to engine driver and in the later years of his service, when the steam engine was phased out, he became an Instructor on the electric trains. He retired in 1981 after 50 years service. Sadly Tom died in January 1994 at the age of 76 years.

Happy at their work. Christine Porter, Jennifer Starkey (nee Mellor) and Evelyn Spencer, packing hampers with stationary at the British Railways Printing factory in 1965. The hampers were loaded onto goods wagons waiting in a siding at the rear of the factory and transported to various railway depots throughout Britain.

Members of the Crewe North Shed breakdown gang, pictured at Leamington Spa on November 21st 1965, after righting engine 75005 ( inset), which had been involved in an accident.

Crewe Locomotive Works Erecting Shop in 1965. Looking a lonely figure as he tours the workshops, George Chaves was over here representing the Bolivian Railways, hoping to place orders for the company. Sadly he died on the plane while returning home.

Sir Oliver Cromwell, the last engine to leave the Crewe Locomotive Works under its own steam, is seen here on the traverse, slowly making its way back into service , after receiving a thorough overhaul in 1967. During a short ceremony to mark the occasion, all employees who had worked on the engine, were invited to take part in a group photograph, fronted by the Mayor, Councillor H.P.Vernon, himself a railwayman, he is seen here leaning out of the cab.

L.M.R. cricketer, the late Jeff Clarke, receiving a presentation from the late Tom Bache, right, the L.M.R. Cricket Club Chairman, in 1969.

The famous "Cornwall" steam engine outside the paint shop in the Crewe Locomotive Works in 1970. The former paint shop area is now the site of the Morrison's store.

The Crewe North Shed breakdown gang pictured on a cold day in 1973, after helping at the Hickton North Staffs level crossing accident.

Albert Mee (centre front), pictured with members of his railway breakdown gang on 23rd November 1976 after receiving his British Empire Medal from the Lord Lieutenant of Cheshire, Lord Leverhulme, on behalf of Her Majesty The Queen, at the Crewe Arms Hotel, Crewe. Originally, Albert was invited to Buckingham Palace to collect his medal, but was refused permission to take his 'gang' with him; he then opted to receive his medal locally. He had been connected with innumerable major and minor incidents over the years including the Hixton level crossing accident in 1968, also a crash at Chester Station. Perhaps one of his most memorable was his work on a sleeping car derailment at Nuneaton. Albert and his crew managed to lift wreckage off a young woman who had been trapped for some time, despite several attempts to free her by the emergency services. "He remained on duty with only short breaks for a total of 90 hours" commented Lord Leverhulme. Albert retired on November 18th 1978. Inset: Albert Mee receiving his medal from Viscount Leverhulme.

Engine 46229 'The Duchess of Hamilton', one of the steam engines saved from the cutters torch, seen here being lifted by a giant crane while having repairs to its bogies, during a visit to the Crewe Loco Works in 1980.

The Chairman and General Manager of the British Railways London Midland Region, Mr M.C.Johnson Esq. C.B.E. is pictured unveiling the plaque to commemorate the opening of the Crewe Training Centre at Webb House in 1966. The centre closed in the 1980's.

British Railways long service award recipients pictured with their gifts after a ceremony at the Electric Traction Depot in 1978.

British Railways apprentices at the Crewe Locomotive Works Apprentice School in 1981. Not all of the names are known, but included on the picture are; Cornes, Bartrum, Prince, Sumner, Cope, Lowndes, Thompson and Stubbs.

All the images are of British Railways Apprentices at the Crewe Locomotive Works Apprentice School in 1981.

British Railways Apprentices at the Crewe Locomotive Works Apprentice School in 1981. Back Row; Mick Roberts, Trevor Bloor, Steve Vickers, ? , Kevin Maloney, Mark Hall, ? , Shaun Wilkinson and Mark Wells. Front row; ? , ? , Mark Ryder, Rob Stretton, Shaun Baker, Richard Wilcox, ?, Alan Langley and Gordon Halford.

With the steam engine now part of history, this D.M.U. ( Diesel Multiple Unit) is seen dropping and picking up passengers at the Nantwich Station on 3rd March 1983. The station buildings have now been converted to a restaurant.

Crewe Works Erecting Shop staff being entertained watching this wrestling match at their 1985 Christmas concert.

A line-up of artists (all employees) who entertained at the Christmas concert in the Crewe Works Erecting Shop in 1985.

The Lion steam engine, seen here at the Crewe Heritage Centre in 1986. Not a product of Crewe, it was bought by the L.M.S. in 1920 and displayed in the Merseyside County Museum, Liverpool. The Lion last came to Crewe in 1947 when it entered Crewe Works for major repairs. Said to be the oldest locomotive in the world, The Lion played the title roll in the film 'The Titfield Thunderbolt'.

# STAGE-STRUCK CREWE

Pretty young ladies posing for a front of house photograph for a charity show at the New Theatre, Heath Street in 1936. Standing; ? James. Seated; Beryl Stubbs and Barbara Westgate.

Chorus Line 1936.

On February 14th to 19th, 1938, The Crewe Secondary School Old Students Association presented A Dutch Musical Incident," Miss Hook of Holland" at the New Theatre, – (Now the Lyceum Theatre) – Crewe. In this scene 'Father I love your tune' is Ivy Picken who played 'Miss Hook of Holland'. Left is Dudley Gilbert (Lieutenant De Coop), Charles H.Latham (Captain Adrian Paap) and Merrick Jones (Bandmaster Van Vuyt).

This is the cast of " Miss Hook Of Holland" which was staged at the New Theatre ( now The Lyceum), Crewe, on February 14th to the 19th, 1938, by The Old Studs Association. Included in the picture are; Percy Fleet, Charles Latham, Dudley Gilbert, Merrick Jones, Maurice Waugh, Fred Marrill, Douglas Howes, G.William Lea, Kitty Brooke, Marjorie Moore, Beryl W. Clarke, Millie Lyons, and Ivy Picken.

The cast of "Bonaventure" staged by 'The Occasional Players' in 1950. Included in the picture are Muriel North, Grace Pugh, John Stubbs, Beryl Heaton, Gavin Bolton, Mrs Melville Simpson and Constance Allen.

Crewe Occasional Players on stage for 'The Importance Of Being Earnest' on October 3rd 1951. Left to right; Beryl Heaton, Nellie Stubbs, Muriel North, Lilian Newton, John F. Stubbs, Louis Townley, Eric Birgwin and William Broady.

Members of the local repertory company who appeared in "The Importance Of Being Ernest" at the Crewe Lyceum Theatre in 1967.

Youngsters from the Yvonne School of Dancing, on stage for a photo call before a show in the early 1970's.

Male members of the cast of 'West Side Story', practising the 'jets and sharks' dance routine, which was staged at the Crewe Lyceum Theatre in the 1970's.

The 'House Full' signs went up at the Lyceum Theatre for every performance of Century Theatre's production of ' A Midsummer Night's Dream', which ran from the 24th to the 27th February 1993. It was the first time since the Borough Council took over the running of the theatre in 1991 that the full run of a drama production was sold out. Pictured are: Left to right, Jeith Hassall, Administrator, Century Theatre, Louise Norman, Press Officer, Century Theatre and Cliff Stansfield, General Manager, Lyceum Theatre.

Members of the cast of 'West Side Story' pictured at rehearsals. These girls, from the Yvonne Dancing School, took part in the show at the Lyceum Theatre in the 1970's.

Nine Years old, Natalie Kent in 1985, the daughter of Peter and Marie Kent who were Mayor and Mayoress of Crewe and Nantwich that year. Not to be upstage by her parents, Natalie appeared in Showtime at the Lyceum Theatre and later in the show "Annie".

Mr Stephen Wischhusen pictured with members of a repertory company outside the Lyceum Theatre. Mr Wischhusen and his company, Garrick House had managed the theatre for a seven year period ending in January 1991. This picture shows the front of the theatre prior to its alteration in 1994.

The Widows Alms Houses, Welch Row. The building was converted from three 16th century cottages in 1676 and six widows lived there. It will perhaps be remembered more recently as the Cheshire Cat, an eating house opened in 1962 serving the best English food. In 1972 it was opened as a disco club but later closed through lack of support. The smile has since been put back on the face of the Cheshire Cat. After standing derelict for a few years it has again been developed into a top pub and restaurant.

Love Lane Nantwich as it was in 1917. Much of the property has been demolished or altered since this picture was taken.

An early Crown Hotel poster advertising their services, including ' Modern Hearse and Mourning Coaches'.

Nantwich Square 1888. In the 1970's the graveyard, to the left of this picture, was reduced to allow for the widening of the road in the Pepper Street area; this whole area is now pedestrianised.

Nantwich Square looking towards High Street in the 1940's.

A quiet Shropshire Street, Audlem, in the 1940's.

Prior to pedestrianisation. A double decker bus takes on passengers in Nantwich Square in March 1962.

Nantwich by night. A quiet Friday night in Welch Row in 1974. How times have changed! The Wilbraham Arms public house is the second building on the left.

The Palms Tropical House under construction at the Stapeley Water Gardens in early January 1987. Amazingly, The Palms opened in spring of that year, and has been added to constantly. The Stapeley Water Gardens attracts around a million visitors each year.

Nantwich Fire Brigade around 1908. With this unusual tender belching smoke, I can't tell whether they are starting a fire or putting one out!

Members of the Nantwich Fire Brigade outside their headquarters in Beam Street the 1920's.

This photograph, taken in 1938, shows staff at the Calveley depot of the United Dairies.

The Lord Lieutenant of Cheshire, Viscount Leverhulme (Centre), with the Chairman of the Nantwich Rural Council, Mr A.E.Richardson and councillors and guests during a visit to Stapeley House on February 11th 1950.

Father and son, Harold, left, and Henry Gleave, enjoying a days canal fishing in the 1940's. Harold was the licensee of the Royal Oak public house at Tiverton, Tarporley, for many years.

Fire Officers, Rolf Whittingham (left) and Albert Dean, at work in the old Beam Street Fire Station on 17th October 1959.

V.I.P. Mr Munro visiting the Nantwich Urban District Council Old Peoples' Welfare Centre on 8th July 1961.

Members of the Crewe and Nantwich Badminton Club enjoying a social evening in the Cheshire Cat Barn in 1965.

Office staff at the Nantwich branch of the Vernon Cooper Electrical business pose for the camera in 1965.

His last day at work, Audlem village postman, William Woodhouse, setting out with his final deliveries before his retirement in 1967.

A couple of willing helpers lending a hand at a 1968 style indoor barbeque, - in one of the barns,- at this Young Farmers Rally hoping to keep the young farmers well nourished during their rally competitions.

Don't touch! These youngsters, future Young Farmers Club members, are weighing up the mouth watering entries in the fruit flan competition during a Young Farmers Rally at a Nantwich Farm in 1968.

Pictured during cattle judging at a Nantwich farm, these members are toting up the points while taking part in a Young Farmers Rally competition in 1968.

Whippet owners waiting for the signal to put their dogs into the traps before the start of a carnival whippet race in 1970.

Local girl, Yvonne Ormes, winner of several national beauty titles, is seen here wearing the Miss England sash after winning the title in 1970.

This line of youngsters anxiously await the Carnival procession after claiming this prime viewing area in 1970. The Nantwich Carnival was discontinued many years ago.

Traffic Wardens helping to control the crowd as they push forward, along Nantwich High Street, afraid of missing the carnival procession in 1970.

Nurses and helpers making sure these senior citizens were in a prime position to watch the 1970 Nantwich Carnival parade.

After receiving his retirement gifts in 1974, Council Foreman, Jack Wainwright and his wife pose for a photograph with Council Engineer Frank Scaife, who made the presentation. Looking on are Jack's council yard work colleagues.

Alan Yoxall putting the finishing touches to his magnificent sculpture on 19th July 1976.

Local Councillor Donald Potter with Barbra and Sarah Davies, wife and daughter of owner, Ray Davies, and not forgetting 'Jaffa', the Macaw Parrot, during a visit to the Palms tropical house at the Stapeley Water Gardens in 1988.

Anthony Goldstone from the North West Tourist Board pictured with two of the staff in a 'hands on' exercise, (but only with the snake), during a visit to the Stapeley Water Gardens in 1988.

The Britain in Bloom committee, fronted by the Mayor of Crewe and Nantwich, Councillor Alice Roberts MBE, judging the floral displays outside the Nantwich Church in 1988. Mrs Barbra Davies, wife of the owner of the Stapeley Water Gardens, Nantwich, is nearest to the camera, holding one of the hanging baskets.

An unusual pet, but 'Inkey' the Crow was a bit camera shy and wouldn't pose, so his owner Kevin Smith had to hold him while he had this picture taken on 14 July 1985.

Parents and youngsters patiently wait for the carnival parade to come into sight, while the Red Cross nurse stands by; just in case!

Pretty Lesley Williams with her horse Khan after becoming champion at a local gymkhana in the 1970's.

Alpraham Corinthians F.C. 1922-23. It looks as if the team might have donned their kit for this special picture, (their boots, shorts and shirts are very clean), after winning the trophy, centre front.

Nantwich Square was full to capacity as eager fans welcomed home Wilf White (front left of picture) and his horse Nizfella, they had just returned from the 1952 Helsinki Olympics sporting a gold medal. Nizfella was instantly recognisable in the ring, when jumping he used to kick his back legs high in the air to avoid the fences; a trait which caused many smiles. The winning combination in life, from Burland, Nantwich, were also inseparable in death. Nizfella died at the age of 24 years and was buried at Carden Hall, Wilf died in the late 1980's and left instructions that his ashes were to be buried on top of Nizfella: his wishes were complied with. Wilf White's name was added to the Crewe and Nantwich Sporting Roll of Honour in 1994.

Nantwich Cricket team pictured at the Whitehouse Lane ground before taking part in a match in the late 1960's.

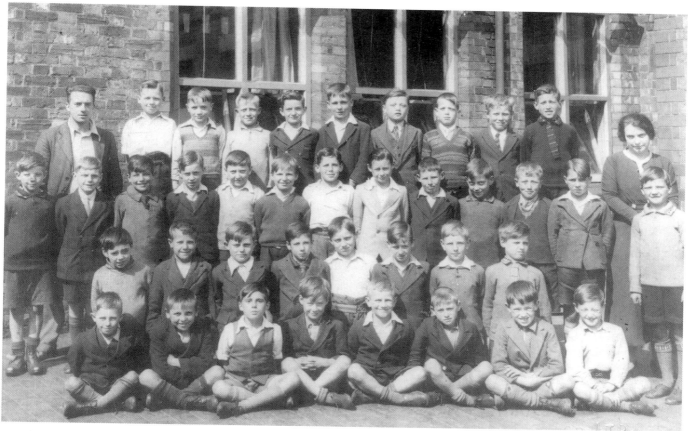

Pupils from the Nantwich Church Lane School in the 1940's.

Another class of pupils of the Church Lane School, Nantwich pictured in the 1940's.

U. D. C. Chairman, Mr Joe Blagg with his wife and members of his family at the Chairman's Ball on 22nd October 1960.

Members of the Acton Operatic Society as they appeared in the original production of "The Arcadians" at the Nantwich Town Hall in 1936. From left to right: D.Muckley (Mrs Smith), R.Manuel (Bobbie), G.Boyer (Eileen), E.Boyer (Jack), M.Voigt (Sombra), L.Boughey (Sir George), R.Walker (Percy) and J.Furnival (Chryses).